God in His Slippers

D0862956

Rod Picott

MEZCALITA PRESS, LLC
Norman, Oklahoma

Cover Design: Stacie Huckeba

MEZCALITA PRESS, LLC
Norman, Oklahoma

God in His Slippers

Table of Contents

Acknowledgements

Buckets of thanks to:
Nathan Brown
Ashley Brown
Stacie Huckeba
Slaid Cleaves
Lloyd R Picott
Lois R Picott
Tasha Thomas
Amanda Shires
Jennifer Tortorici
Jim Harrison
Nicholson Baker
Mary Gauthier

Special thanks to Jerry Daniels for starting the fire
all those years ago and for forgiving my
penmanship, grammar and spelling.

God in His Slippers

Rod Picott

On the Road at 50

The damn loneliness is unrelenting.
You laugh at their jokes
from a few bar stools down and you think
well maybe…
she seems nice…
and you try to catch her eye.
But in the end, it's the flickering blue
of the television
to thrum you to sleep
and not the strange turbulent air of a new kiss.

You check the tires,
scan the fm then the am signal looking
for just-one-good-song.
You gather the trash from the floorboards and
think you will feel reborn.
You wait wait wait to play the songs
you know you will be inside of –
the songs you hope will make you seem
less of a prick and more human.

You are grateful and sometimes you are not.

Like a lone strange fish in the deep
you are making your way in slow motion
with only the scarcest bits of life available –
only your own touch
to calm yourself
from the chaos of the ocean.

How to write:

You have to show up.
You have to be there when the flint slaps
the oxygen and fuel together
and the thing can ignite.
You have to blow gently until it starts to glow
and then feed it.
You feed it until it's roaring
red hot and scary as hell
then keep shoving logs into the pit
until it's sucking all the oxygen
back in on itself.
Then you get your tools out and go to work.
That's how you write.
But first you have to show up.
A pencil and some paper help too.

A Small Inheritance

The boots never fit.
The boy's bones were small
then too big overnight.

Once there was room to stomp
comically around the floor – a walrus
in the kitchen.
Suddenly the heel box was tight and constricting
and his short lifetime of collected advice –
"If you have your health you have everything." –
was let go like pollywogs from a Mason jar.

And he could see
more clearly in the corners
of the older man's eyes
fear of the world
with its math, salesmen,
tollbooths that need quarters, estimates,
checkbooks, lust, leaking pipes,
revenge, alimony and constant small betrayals.

And seeing this was a gift
that the boy cobbled
into his own – now well-worn – boots.

To Ann: With Whom I Once
Caught Fireflies

A woman growing older stares
at a photograph in a silver frame
longing more for what will never be
than what was.

She buried a child.
A small driving mistake
was made on a back road
near the place
where I knew her years ago.

The boy will never
outgrow the hockey jersey
that has slowly given up the ghost
of his cheap cologne.

This is the wrong order.
We should bury our parents.
This is a thing
no one should know.

The Weatherman

Life grows smaller,
becomes a series of tasks
dictated by the portly weatherman
on the television screen.
He will let you know
if the lawn can be mowed,
prescription can be filled,
the mail can be sent,
cans of beans can be bought
(even though there is a wartime hoarding
of them behind
the pressboard cupboard door).

The weatherman is in charge now.
He hands over the keys
to the tractor.
There was a moose rubbing his face
on the side view mirror
of the truck.
A squirrel was executed
for stealing from the chickadees.
The lawn chair folds out.
The lawn chair folds up.
The only thing
the weatherman is not in charge of
is when his whiskers are shaved,
his hair clipped into a rusted dust pan.
The weatherman is even in charge
of when you listen to the weatherman –
which is often.

I Don't Think of Her

I don't think of her.
Except when I do.
And then that dark river
pulls hard
and the rushing water in my head
erases everything in its path.

Her long fingers.

Her dusky hair smell.

Her lily voice.

And the place between her legs
where she gave up the mystery
of the world
and I received it all –
the smallest sweet breath
and the rage of devouring.

Then all I can think of.
Is her.

A Love Letter to a Song

A song propped great oak beams in the basement
and allowed me to move
with chaos and abandon on the floors above.

It healed my suffering mind
and gave me a thief's courage.

A song took a battered and bruised heart
and filled it flush with coursing dark red blood.

Limbs bound were loosed and the great sky
filled my lungs.

The notes have changed. The chords are fingered
more delicately now.
But those oak beams—old, dried,
cracked open now
haven't
          moved
                    an inch.

New York City Part 1

I was a teenager the first time I saw her.
My buddy John and I combed dirty record stores
looking for bootleg records
of Bruce Springsteen and The Who.
At night while his parents drank and laughed
with somebody's relatives
we schemed
to get our hands on some booze.

A taut film played out
in every piss stinking subway ride.
Strangers barked indecipherable instructions.
There were glorious golden Latin girls
so ripe and strong I folded in on myself
and counted up every single thing
I did not know and I counted
for a long fucking time.
At least I knew that I *didn't know*.
That was something at least.

Lost and wandering the streets
took a cheap knife
and carved away everything familiar
leaving a wobbly legged kid
where I had stood.
Welcome to the new world.
She's dressed in fishnet stockings
and a police hat
and she looks you right in the eye buddy.
She's not waiting for you to ask her to dance.
She doesn't give a shit if you want to dance.

She is the dance.

We never saw anyone famous.
Everyone looked famous to us
in our Levi's from the mall
and our haircuts
that our mothers gave us.

Six hours away
a dog lay sleeping
on a linoleum floor
dreaming of chasing a stick.

Mother

She was only a child herself
when she made her first.
She cleaned up after her own wedding
with her future curled inside her belly.
A few months later
there he was – cross-eyed
and screaming for the world to hear.
She did her best
with no tools.
No one bothered to lend her a shovel.
She dug with her hands to raise him.
Sixty years later
you can still see the dirt
under her nails
and the worry
in her eyes.

Time

No compass can tell you.
You only know
by the jealous mirror's sad sneer
and the labor of limbs
and by the imperceptibly lessened torpidity
of your pride.

When will the last leaf fall?
We all ask.

But while you stand patiently watching
there on the stained deck
for the cold bony finger of your winter wind
to loose the leaf…

Behind you a young fox with golden eyes
sinks his flashing teeth into a mole,
wasps flurry,
and a small green thing reaches even now
deep into the dark earth to find
what no compass can chart.
Time.

Entangled

Her limbs wrapped in mine –
entwined like some ancient
and strange animal ritual
that went on until there was no telling
which wet gift came from whom.
The whole of the night sky
went on about its business
and we went about ours.
A New Orleans whore would have blushed.
Every trace was covered, uncovered and
abandoned
spent for the next taking.
The glory of untethered need –
ungracious and unbartered
and taken like found treasure.
Begging desire given and accepted
in full throated swallows.
Desire like oxygen and just as flammable.
We were flame throwers burning
each other clean of our private sins.
We were sentient stars hurling blinding light
from the past into the future.
I left her scent on me an entire day
and was a blind and mad dog
at every rediscovery of her on me.

Clutter

I live in one room –
two if I count the bathroom.
The place is filled with things:
books, records, CDs, a few pieces
of furniture to drape my bones across
after I drink wine.

It seems to me
that we fill up whatever space we have
with things.
I decided to live
in a very small space
so I only need a few things.
And still there are more things
than I need here.

Inside me though
the room is not filled.
There is no comfortable place inside me
to rest my bones after the wine.
She's *out there* somewhere.

Jealousy

I am a cat crouched
in the tall grass
all twitching muscle
and narrow green eyes
as the beautiful leopard
climbs the tree with my catch.

He Only Cried Twice

Only twice has your father cried –
once when his mother died,
once when I asked him for a divorce.
My mother said this quietly
as though it were a small betrayal.

But one time when I was a child
I was watching
a film called "The Miracle Worker."
I was sitting very close to the television.
A blind girl was running
from thing to thing.
She had discovered language
through her hands.
It was beautiful to see.
I heard a strange sound behind me.
I turned my head
to the soft animal sound.
And there on the sofa
I saw my father,
choking back his tears.
His face contorted.

I said nothing
and quickly turned away.
My father, that tough shell,
with his Marines tattoos
crying at the sight of a young blind girl,
the world – a brilliant explosion
at her fingertips.
I never told a soul.

But my mother was wrong.
I wonder where the other tears fell.
Surely there were more
though they disappeared silently
somewhere out there in the world.
People are more than you think
I think.

Doubt

I'm not smart enough
to be a good poet.
I'm only smart enough
to build a tarpaper shack
that fails to keep the rain
from the lawnmower.
Then, there is such trouble
getting the motor to start.

Other poets have exotic tools
built for the grandest piling
and the finest carving.
They build masterpieces –
worthy of sanctity.

While I yank at the pull starter and curse.

A Delicate Question

I asked her to let me know
when she had her time.
Because I was nervous.
The way you get when you are a single man
and have had a big time one night.
Then the next days you think
maybe you shouldn't have had
quite such a big time that night.

Being not much of a gambler
you would think I'd hedge my bets.
But the curves of her
had their way with me and so
we had our way with each other
and had a big night.

I felt like a heel asking her.
And of course she was wondering
about the same thing but
in a very different way.
So my request was received
with some hurt feelings.

When her time came I felt relieved and also
guilty about my relief.
I wonder what all of this means…
what it says about me, about her
and about the nature of these
delicate dances that come
after the very indelicate dance.

Aging

The roar is dying slowly.
In its place
there is settling down in the soft grass
a mute and toothless beast.
His long sinewy limbs are still strong
but now you must come quite near
for him to reach your flesh.
The days of the chase are over.

His eye still sees the fast twitch of the tail
above the tips of grass.
His mouth still salivates at the thought.
But the grass is so soft.
And the chase has gone on
for so very long now.

Church

Reverend Blankenship was the minister and
my mother said we were Episcopalian.
I'm not sure what the distinction is but
it's a good word and I liked to say it.

It's probably one of those Catholic-light
religions. You know – Catholic without
the Latin, incense and molesting
but I'm not sure.
We stopped going after a while.

When I was a teenager and wrestling with
what kind of person I was going to be
my mouth got me in some trouble but
it was just noise.
I was a good kid even though
the principal didn't like me.

So my father suddenly tried to make me
go to church again with him.
It was very strange.
I didn't do much with my father.
We were at an impasse – I didn't like fishing.
He didn't like Keith Richards.
Lines were drawn between fishing and cocaine.

When I stopped going to church
he went a few times on his own.
My father – in the one suit he's ever owned
sitting alone in church
worrying about me.

But I had a new church of my own by then
and just like it is with new converts
there was no talking me out of it.

In my church there were
guitars hanging on the walls
girls who smelled like incense
gatefold album covers
mystery and exultation
and the feeling that I was finding out
what I believed in.

Machinery

The machines all have their place.
One prints, one sorts, one cuts.
They perform little watchable miracles.

A lawnmower.
Who thought all the blades need to be
one height?
A barber I suspect.
Even the can of wasp spray has a job –
to propel the nasty chemical poison into that
papery Nazi homeland.

Consider the can opener.
It's fairly simple but how the hell else would you
get in there?
I suspect the can and its opener were invented
at the same time.
What kind of idiot would invent a can
then have to invent a door opener for it?

Of course some machines are faulty.
Some explorers wandered around the Arctic
in circles
before they died frozen in their tracks
because they had lead in their brains
from badly designed cans.
A can of peas can kill you.
Imagine what a bad lawnmower could do.

Double Edge

My brother's teacher's husband had drowned.

His last vision: the black clouds
of an angry Atlantic storm
just before he was pulled
under the icy grey water.
The sky, filled with menace,
pushing him down
into the ocean
as his fingers slipped aft.

This is what I saw
in my child's fortune-telling mind.
Tears streamed my cheeks.
An impossible horrible thought
had rooted itself
and would not be unburied.
Hours I wept in my pajamas
with the vision of his death.

Now it seems strange.
But looking back
I see the first terrifying betrayal
of my imagination.
To be born with a machine so capable
of ecstasy and horror.
The shocking details of
the white-hot spark of
vision and empathy
are a very sharp blade.

I can see him still,
eyes wide with panic
as his white knuckles
lose their wet hold.

My chest still rises slightly
at the thought.
I swallow. It tastes of salt water.

Ex Lover

You know her secret places,
the wonders of her geometry,
the heartbreaking childhood memory,
the sharp breath of her slow morning rise.
You've seen her self-delusion.
She knows that you have seen it
and she has seen your failure.
You know she knows you know she knows.

There was that time
when your back was broken.
She carried all the things on that trip –
like a sure footed little mule.
There is no need for hush money.
There are some conspiracies
you will carry to your dirt bed.

There is all this in silence
as you eat your salad
and talk about getting new tires.

Cold War

The Dostoevsky
sits ignored under
the Jim Harrison.
Jim was a big guy.
I wonder if Fyodor feels suffocated
under there?
I'm told Dostoevsky has mined
the deepest veins of the human mind –
uncovered the most intimate
rural paths of our thinking,
motivations and desires.

But Christ he prattles on –
I got it Fyodor –
get on with it for Christ's sake.
And he doesn't tell me anything
about the trees or birds.
He doesn't mention the coyotes.
It's nice to know which birds are overhead
even under all that fur-hatted melancholy.

Sleep

She used to arrive with whales.
Now she swims in with minnows.
There are glorious drugs of course,
but they leave you
feeling like you had a version of sleep
but not the original version
by the original artist.

Once my eyes lolled about in dreams so filthy
my body gave in and washed itself of them
into my sheets.
Now my dreams are broken shards of a pane
giving nothing of the whole. Worthless.
Dear sweet sleep once wiped the chalkboard clean
and brought reckless troubles
of her own invention.
Now she's lost her will
and marvelous gift of imagination.

Or did I?

It's Not That Kind of Thing

She's small but long.
The body of a high school freshman
who plays sports,
a crooked and toothy smile that's
awkward happy and sexy sad,
a grown woman in the frame of a foal.

From her I coax nearly crying orgasms
so lovely and big they break
like thunderheads and just as wet.
The smell of her on my fingers
makes me hard again.
I am 51 so I'm seldom hard again
and wonder when the last one will be
and worry about it too.

Her hair is a rumor of brown,
so fine and breezy.
Scars on her skin here and there
make me wonder
but I don't ask.
It's not that kind of thing.

She can't pay attention, even to herself,
so she talks
from one thing to the next and
I can't follow – the talk always backtracking
to pick up a proper noun
so I know who the hell she's on about.

I can quiet her with a touch
and her body starts the steep ramp
of the roller coaster again.
I want her and I want to be alone.
Because it's not that kind of thing.

In the morning she dresses silently,
a skinny ghost who leaves a dark coffee
near the night table
for me to wake to
and kisses my slack and sleeping mouth.
Except I'm not sleeping.
Because it's not that kind of thing.

I should tell her.
But she doesn't want me to tell her.
She already knows it's not that kind of thing.

Gung No

This hotel bed is good enough
that I simply want to lie here.
The television is not on.
It's too early and I haven't had any liquor yet.
The book near me has nothing to say today.
The guitar gets played every night.

The softening of the day has begun.
But the night time when I work
hasn't crept into the room yet.

So I would say I'm just drifting
here on the bed
like Dustin Hoffman on the pool float
in The Graduate.
I'm not like De Niro in Raging Bull.
There is nothing raging.
I'm just waiting
for the light outside my window
to tell me it's time
to be exciting.

The Trouble with Art

He asked if the problem with him
is that he has no demons to conquer
and carve into art.

I've been thinking about it.
If you are going to be good at sewing
you will need a lot of torn clothing to repair or
poverty stricken friends.

And if you want to be a great mechanic
your back lawn will need a graveyard of rust.

That is unless you are a puzzle solver.
If it's simply math to you
then I suppose
you might manage to imitate art quite well.

But you ain't gonna be Leonard Cohen –
howling softly with a greasy wrench
in his hand
as he turns the bolt free.

A Polaroid of a Pirate

In the Polaroid I ran hard,
pedaled furiously,
was too tall,
and too thin.
There were small sores on my
face neck and back.
My ribs poked through
like a chicken
ready to be cooked.
I was unattractive
but managed a few years later
to have a sweet funny girlfriend.
She was pretty
and we unlocked the hushed secrets together.
Each with our own key –
we turned them simultaneously
on the treasure chest.
The priceless riches we unlocked
poured over us.
Over and over we plundered.

Big Man on an Airplane

The baritone so big and brassy
Sales! Man! Tales to some young lassie
Her eyelids giving up the drop
Does he notice? Not
But bellows forth to entertain us!
Something of an airplane walrus
And swirling in his great round boredom
An ear can hear his cracking worth
And see it in expanse of girth
Where once a kid could find no ear
And so he knows not how to hear

Himself.

Bird of Prey

In the old photograph
he is young and hard.
He's standing next to a howitzer.
His job then was to fire
the brutal, massive gun.
There is baby fat on his shaven face and
grease under his fingernails.

He is surrounded by friends.
They all fired the howitzers together.
He has the devil in his eyes
and a tattoo of an eagle's talons
inked into his arm.

In the new photograph he is
a bent reed straining
and leaning on a rusty lawn chair.
No friends are in the new photograph,
just a skinny dog who never leaves his side.

The devil has left his eyes now –
replaced with the reflection
of an endless blue sky.

A bird of prey is perched –
barely visible
in the tree line behind him.

The Box

There are days,
for no particular reason that I can figure,
when I simply want to dump the box over,
smack the bottom to loose anything stuck
to the cardboard there
and start the whole goddamn thing over.

I'd like to fill the box with different stuff.
I'd put in a lot of hard work,
a lot of lovers
(even the same ones that were in the box before)
more books,
more films that were made between
1967-1975,
more movement
and more conversation where I want to hear
what the other person is going to say next...

It's not regret that I'd like to dump out
but all the wastefulness.
All that worrying took up a lot of space
and the wanting too.

I'll trade all the want and worry for some doing,
laughing, fucking and love.
Straight up trade—whattya say?

Dover NH

You R-dropping oaks.
You plaid-shirted dance club.
You cheap as pine needles sonofabitch.
Who fills your thrift stores?
Did you sell the brown coat for a quarter
to buy the black coat for a dime?

I question your motives,
your automotive advice,
and your pizza most of all.
You serve that grease wheel
looking right into my eyes
knowing I don't know
your Greek from Italian.

"Soundsaboutright Buddy.
Fucking A – this ain't Massachusetts."
We don't parse neighborhoods
by cured meats.
This is New Hampshire.
We can't tell your salami
from your mortadella.
Here we swing hammers,
buy lottery tickets,
drive to state liquor stores,
feed our dogs,
fight with our fists,
know what duct tape is for
and spit on the coffee breaks of union guys.
"Spit right the fahk ahn em. Fucking pussies."

"I got Bacahdi and a mega bucks numbah
aftah work wud u do?"

I left. That's what I did.
But still sometimes I think about a girl
from Vermont and her chestnut hair,
and a third-floor apartment
where I did another man wrong
but drenched myself in the mercy
only a chestnut haired girl
from a broken home in Vermont
knows how to bestow.
I wore a plaid shirt to the dance club
the night I met her.

Fuckinarightbuddy.

Camera

In the soft focus lens of distant memory
you are beautiful.
Your soft brown hair
your small firm roundness
your strong pretty smell like the outdoors.

But when I squint hard
and turn the ring on the lens
I see your unforgiving heart pumping
like a small fist
and I think it's good I have a quality lens
for my camera.

Uncle Louis

He came in the summers
with his horse-toothed wife.
Stayed far too long.
He'd been a state trooper,
the perfect job
for someone with angry blood.

He refused to eat at the table.
He ate standing
at the stained Formica kitchen counter
with his indecipherable resentments.

He was raised by a preacher
who spilled all of his inherited treasure
before he could get his hard fist on it.

I shook his hand once
when I was twelve.
I had learned
that I should shake hands very firmly.
And so I did.
He took offense
then crushed my hand
with his state trooper fist
until my one of my thin white bones popped.

Tears came to my eyes
and I saw a slight smile crease his dark face.
I squeezed as hard
as I could for as long as I could
until he won.

Then I went to my bedroom
and cried like a child would.
And he was pleased with himself
having retrieved some coin of his stolen treasure.

Wyoming

This golden sands place
with its rocky fists punching on itself,
is in the fingers of no river or forest.

Its great yawning sky swallows the world.

Pale Rider plays across your windshield and
the dust finds every – single – hidden – crack.

What the hell do they do for work
on the moon?
How do they afford these new pickup, pickup,
(excuse me) pickup trucks?

The regular stores don't bother here.
I'll bet it's the math that's the problem.
And so there is some novelty.
Don't get me wrong – it's the same crap sold
but a different salesman.

The wind is eternal
in the vast non-peopled-ness
of this planet with the Indian name.

Believer

I'm nearly always filled
with self doubt.
I believe I'm unworthy and
without talent.
But what if I'm wrong?

No More Grease

Her:
She labels cans and jars
with wide pieces of white tape.
Black marker shouts the contents at you:
BEANS
or
COFFEE CREAMER
or
CRYSTAL LIGHT.
This is old age for her –
that a thing must be restated
in black ink to make it so.
Pleasures are few and small
as the ivory stitch in a ruffled curtain.

Things are not good here now.
But we pretend that the sunshine
is very fine today
and that this old place with its hard water,
flooding basement
and sagging floor
is a serving of heaven from God's own
pie knife.

Him:
His memory is cracked now
and slowly leaking the 76 years away
out into the thin Maine air.
Even he can hear the elusive hiss.
Alex Rodriguez is retiring today

and I mention this only to mark this day
as the day when I recognize
that the gears, long rusted
are beginning to grind to a halt
and there is no grease left in the can.

Old Books

There are ruddy, fingered pages
chewed through long ago
when these words became alive
for the first time.

Blood ran, lovers suffered
and schemers schemed
across the dog-eared pages
of a writer's desires –
tracing them so finely
as to be left not knowing
the first from the last
or the dove from the cloth.

And long as enumerated
and its organized stain
of small bones visible,
its light remains lit
for whomever wishes
the warmth of flame it offers.

Walking the Beige Carpet
of the Long Hotel Hallway

Walking the beige carpet
of the long hotel hallway
with small slow steps
our arms brushed briefly
and ever so lightly
almost imperceptibly
with geometry so fine
as to be immeasurable
by rule or any known math.

A spark flamed to full howl below
and blood – iron rich
and hard as a high white river –
flooded its banks and I asked her,

"Did you feel that?"

From her beautiful freckled constellation:

"Yes."

The Train You Ride

Your mother once gave you a store-bought
dessert
for the triumph of a report card
that contained all A's.
Forty years later you stand in the doorway with an
open hand
still waiting for your swiss roll.

Your father once belted your ass
for smart mouthing
when his belly was full of Schlitz.
This was the wrong time to smart mouth and
decades later
you are still making sure you get the timing
of your smart mouth right.

You can't believe the dessert the world brings you
unless you are willing to accept
the ass whipping as well.
Why should one be the truth
and the other false?
Who are you to choose?

Neither of these people standing before you
are truthful
unless both of them are.
You don't get to choose.
But of course you choose.

And which person you hear
says everything about you –
if you lick your sugary fingers
or rub your sore red ass –

and which train you will arrive on.

Extra Blanket

In the morning
regret hangs in the air
like alcohol and ashtrays.
I was an animal in need.
She was too.
But now the lack of that other
deeper thing
makes a crease
in the perfect smooth morning.

She brought coffee.
I pretended to sleep
as she set it down
beside my head.
She went back to sleep.
What a sweet offering –
to bring coffee to the bed stand
of such a ragged animal
and his small deceptions.

Her head barely peaks
from the extra blanket
she spread on top of herself.
She felt cold.
I understand.

Home

I always want to go.
I always want to leave.
So I'm looking for a sort of shell
I can wear like a turtle.
He seems to be home.

I finger though the mail.
I toe around the place.
The braided rug is nice
and I installed an expensive sink
with a nice trademark stamped onto it
in a classy grey and beautiful font.
There are some drugs, some records
and books I like,
but where is the home exactly?
The roof doesn't leak so that's all fine.
And the water comes out of the pipes just fine
then goes back down just fine.
But I'm still looking around the place
for home.
Maybe I'll flatter myself and describe elegantly
and romantically
how the road is my home.
But that is a hack of a lie
And not really worth spending time on.
Lies should be made of bigger stuff.
I'm an astronaut. There's a good one.

A Russian spent 400 something days in space.
Did he bring his records and braided rug?
Was it anticlimactic when he got home?

"Look at all my mail. Here are all my things.
Maybe I should'a stuck with that view I had
the last year.
I can't see shit out these windows..."

When I leave I always clean first,
then it's nice when I get back.
That's the sort of person I am.
Then I walk in and say, "I live in a nice place.
Very clean in here."
Then I look out the window and wonder
if my home is out there somewhere.

Choices

Make something.
Break something.
Or listen to the birds sing.
That's all you get to choose from.

Two Dancers and a Leopard

She was lithe and had all the ease of nature,
the effortless bend of a green snake in the
summer grass
or a dorsal fin cutting salty water.

I, on the other hand,
had the grace of stones
descending a steep footpath
or the hikers scattering below.

She desired someone else.
Her body ached for the boy with black boots
who moved like her, in time with her,
and wore his full brass for the world to see.
It was all that hard muscle she craved
and all that careful carelessness of cool
draped across his geometry.

So I gave her what I had.
I made her coffee in the morning.
I let her tell me about her desire for him.
…and I didn't blink.
I left her interior world alone and didn't try to
move the furniture.
I didn't ask her to move his picture from the wall
– I never moved a thing.
And so for those years
of her beautiful aching youth I was there
washing her coltish body down
and holding the slender fingers of her hand

as she crossed the stream
and never trying to rearrange
the rooms inside her mind.
And dancing the best I could.

And now we are all older.
And maybe she wonders.
And maybe he wonders.
But there are things I know now,
that he'll never know,
because I knew back then
what he didn't know.

A leopard can sometimes steal the soft
beating flesh away from a tiger.

The One Who Watches Me

Who are you?
What is your motivation – you inside there?
What gear is being greased and to what end?
Are you jealous?
Are you vain?
I'm watching you very closely.
You won't get away with it next time.
I have video machinery whirring away
in a locked closet
and there is a black box
recording every false move, forced smile
and avoidant glance.
You will be brought to high court and
punishments meted out for your treasons.
Even this one, you self-conscious
self-admonishing fool.
You won't get away with this…
or this…

The Coyote

The coyote laid herself down
in the green grass
behind my suburban house.
I stood on the deck, leaning crooked
with my broken back, and
looked right into her yellow eyes.

She looked back at me, suspiciously.
I felt a strange connection to the animal.

Then she stood wearily
and with an injured leg
limped into the dark woods –
a look of worry in her eyes
for all the world that is strange to her blood
and getting too close.

Birthday Cake

She is elegant in her black dress.
She knows how to pick them now
and she is sleek and sophisticated.
Back when I loved her
she dressed like a birthday cake –
too much of everything:
eyelashes, cleavage, ruffles, feathers,
whatever could be added on.

Now she is glamorous.
Back when I loved her
she was a child,
ruddy-faced,
baby soft and impossibly pretty but
not yet elegant.

We spoke in a code of our own invention
like lost twins in a forest surviving on berries.
Now she is married to a good strong man,
has a child of her own
and of course she is older
and maybe that's made the difference.

Either way I'll always
think of her
as a lovely piece of birthday cake
so sweet in my mouth.
But I couldn't survive
on something so sweet
so I had to put the paper plate down.

When I looked up again
she was champagne in a crystal flute.
But I'll bet she still talks like west Texas
and dreams in colorful parties
and remembers a few clicks
of our secret code.
That is a very nice thought.

Tired of Myself

Yes.
I am.

Luggage

My mother liked her children to be ill.
Then she could be even more of a mother.
She could prepare elixirs, heal and give empathy –
I suspect the empathy she never received.
She had a rattle of a psychology
there in her head
broken bits all disconnected from each other.

Why would people make children
then raise them to be broken?
Oh that's right...
In time you will give what you receive.

When I was a boy, I used to wonder
about those kids you could tell
were already broken.
Why didn't anyone step in to remove
their collars and give them love?
They sat in their chairs
with dirty fingernails and
cloudy eyes downcast
making sure to catch no one's eye.

Some of the girls took to sex,
some of the boys took to fists.
These were broken kids
who still had fight inside
to take back what was stolen from them.

And we wonder
why some people are assholes.
What nerve we have to question them when
we are all complicit in their making – one small
cruelty at a time.
Imagine what some people have to carry.

Oceans

His drinking was a problem.
The Atlantic was not enough.
He swallowed oceans
of the stuff until it washed clean
the person that he was.
It rinsed clear all the dirt
from his windshield but
then he couldn't see
through the storm.
He couldn't drive his life anymore
and went skidding sideways into the gutter.

Now he's on the road again.
But the car is damaged –
out of alignment.
He has to drive more carefully.
It takes longer to get where he's going.
He keeps stopping
to get out
and look at the damage
and he wonders
if he'll arrive
where he was trying to go.

Bastard

I was a real bastard that time
when I chased that girl with a stick and shouted
"Witch! Witch!"
Someone else was there too.
I think his name was Danny.
And he shouted "Witch! Witch!" too.

It felt like pretend and then it didn't.
I looked into her eyes
and saw something horrible –
my own reflection.

And now I think to myself
the reflection of that boy
is the thing I see in the cruelty of men.
I wonder if they discover their cruelty
in simple play?
It's a terrifying thought.

Old and Older

It started hard.
You had to put it on full choke,
then drop it to half choke.
Pull the cord,
over and over.
But even if it coughed to life,
it had become too heavy for him.
He's getting old.

So I bought him a smaller chainsaw.
It starts easier.
And he gets to tear into trees
like he did years ago –
all sunburned forearms
and empty beer cans on the ground.
I felt like a real grown man,
to see him smaller in this way.

I took the old saw back to Tennessee.
Then found to my surprise,
it is too heavy for me too.

Investing Time

I've been a disappointment to her.
She came here for my attention
but my attention waned.
It's not that my attention
was anything special.
I listen.
I hear her voice and the stories it brings.
Anyone who wants to get along with people
can listen.
That's a simple thing.
You just listen to the words.
But she had something else in mind.
A longer project
with more input on my part.

Mornin' Sam

The woodpecker tapped out a message
in his crazy
upholstery tack code.
Tip tip tip then
tip then
tip tip.
It is time to wake up.
So I opened the screen door
to let him know I was up now
for Christ's sake.
He was wearing a suit that reminded me of an
Oreo cookie.
He acknowledged me
then went off to work.
I did the same.

Tattoo

On my knees – face filled with tears
I begged like a child for more time.

She swiveled easily back to the blue screen
and shook her head gently.
"No… What's wrong with your breath?"
"I can't eat."
"It's terrible."
"Yes, I know."

And so there is no need for the tattoo.
It's already there.

Gratitude

I'm an ungrateful sort.
I have mix tapes
and books and handmade
collages and cards.
People must have spent hours
on these things.

But the gifts go into the scatter
of what little ephemera I allow and
their authors are lost to me
unless they've scribbled their name on them.

So it occurs to me
that while I act the part in the moment
in the end I'm an ungrateful sort.

Or is it possible my trunk is simply full and
while traveling I can't be burdened
with any more trinkets?
That's a nice way to put it.

I would like to be a collector
like Tom Waits
or my ex-lover Alicia
who once said
"let's fill our cabin with things we love."

After we filled the cabin with things we loved
she decided I wasn't one of the things
(though she kept the mechanical wind-up
woodpecker).

Maybe I should have signed my name on myself.
Maybe she forgot I was the one
who gave me to her or
maybe there was just too much damn clutter.

I'm an ungrateful sort I suppose.
I wonder if maybe everyone is secretly
like this or are there people
who really treasure the things
that fill their cabin?

An Interior Life

In here it all goes according to the plan.
And then suddenly not at all to the plan.
I watch myself.
What is your motivation?
Moving your limbs through the strange outer
world is the only way.
Inside *everything* happens
but nothing *happens*.

So you learn to place your boots
where the footprints are
and note the direction of the little arrows.
He's Denney Terrio and he taught
John Travolta how to dance.
So you watch and try.

Work and Salvation

I picked up Danny Miller in my Blazer.
He had a small truck but I liked driving
and anyway his apartment was on the way.
He chewed tobacco
which was a novelty to me
but I was awfully careful
about which coffee was mine.

We worked like thunder.
"Put some ass into it son," said Danny
who had more ass to put into it than me.
He had a solid middleweight fighter's frame
and animal eyes that went right through you
when he told you a story.

My favorite story was
when he put a carpet knife against
the contractor's throat after throwing him
to the ground,
his bigger partner kicking closed the car door
while the Mexicans
watched like children from the backseat of the
contractor's Buick.
The contractor cut him another check.
You could tell
he would have been dangerous still
if he'd not found Jesus.

He showered often
but rarely washed his clothes which
sort of defeated the purpose.
But he was the kind of guy
you really wanted on your side
when there was trouble
with the other trades.
He'd say, "Why would I have to hit him
when all I need to do is look at him."
It was a statement not a question.

The other story I liked
was when he found salvation.
He'd sat still as a stone in a Texas field
as the bunting and banners flapped in the wind
around him –
the other believers from the revival
having gone away.
He sat for two days – eating nothing and praying
for forgiveness
from carpet knives and his own animal eyes.
As he wilted and his prayers grew bizarre,
a stranger appeared with a box
of fried chicken.
And he was saved
by fried chicken.

Some people really do need to find Jesus
if only to have a place
to get a better set of directions.
Some people start out with bad directions.

Things Have Changed

I started soft.
A green philodendron –
long and skinny
with big hands and feet.
I wanted music, words
and photographs poured into me.

I saw the curve of her neck
where they saw the hills of her sweater.
They were tougher then
with their sports and balls and fights.
All that endless counting
and scoring and winning and losing.
But they couldn't last.
They spent it all in their youth.

And now I sleep with their wives
and daughters.
Now I'm rail thin but hard.
And I eat wild in the grass
while their greasy hands fumble
in the potato chip bag
and search for the remote.
Things have changed.

Longing

I long to lie beside a fine skinned thing –
her sweetness filling my inward breath,
that musky rain air between us.

Not a girl or a woman but that fine perfect
place between
where hope, desire and sparking intellect collide
so beautifully together and ring
the bright bells of the very moment.

Long full kisses
unafraid and greedy
pulling life from me while simultaneously
brimming my body with newness,
senses full sail and filled
with a hard Atlantic salty wind.

She would curl her limbs into mine
and my vine to her.
That soft and steady thrush
of quickening breath
would take forever.
My blood runs for this.

In its promise,
held at arm's length from me here and now,
there is a not yet forgotten sense
of wonder.

Old Friends

My old friend John
is now both of the things
this first line could mean.
He has a new hip.
And so part of him is not him anymore
and not old at all.
His hip is brand new.

He was a tough kid,
never backed down from a fight,
took up boxing for a short time.
They thought it would be good for him.
But he was too big and too strong
for his age so it didn't work out.
You can't have a 13-year-old kid
fighting a 19-year-old man.
The math is wrong and adds up to trouble.

We were good friends –
listened to records together in his
basement room –
the Eagles, Bruce Springsteen,
those two really good Rod Stewart records.
He was funny as hell and
his mother was very kind to me.
She told me once it was good
that I was skinny
because I would look good in disco clothes.
She's gone now to memory.
I think she knew I was struggling
to find which boots I was supposed to wear.

I'm guessing my old buddy John
was struggling to find his boots too.
His father put up with me I think mostly,
but was also very kind
and a good man with ice blue eyes.
We were not exactly outcasts
but not an easy fit either.
I suppose that bonds some people –
like pack animals.

So now he has a new hip.
I have a back like a rattlesnake
that drops its fangs into me
every few months
and leaves me a wobbly mess.
We are old friends.

He's living with a woman who we both
lusted over
when we were just kids
and she was a girl.
She's good to him.
He deserves it.
We went our separate ways
in most ways
a long time ago –
but not all ways.
There remains that long thin wire
that connects you to the distant past
and the people who were there
to help you navigate

those hard lands when you didn't know
which boots to wear.

He has a new hip,
a beautiful partner,
a welding machine and a straight right
you would not want to find yourself on the wrong
end of.
I have a rattlesnake back,
an old guitar
and a lot of pens and paper.
We both have boots that fit now.

Neighbor Girl

We stayed out late –
our wiry arms outstretched
to catch fireflies
then put them in a canning jar
but mostly to touch each other
secretly.

My arm was around her skinny waist.
Her corn silk blonde hair
brushed my neck in the dark.
The summer – our humming conspirator.

Milo Maine

There is no need for dressing up
for any occasion.
There are no occasions here
except for what you decide
is an occasion.
"It's been a long time since I wore this."
The world has no eye on this place
with its pallets and kerosene tanks
and cars for sale – $300.
The distance from camouflage to Kardashian
is the parking lot of the Rite-Aid
then it's back into hiding.

Winter is impossibly long here
and there is a season of mud and black flies
just before the summer begins
and then the blue sky immediately cools
into fall like aluminum foil
wrapped around a baked potato.

Satellite dishes cling to houses like koalas lost
in a strange land.
There is no use for artifice here
and so there is none.
A pizza is a pizza and a tail light is $6.
Good makeup sells like lighter fluid in hell – but
beer?
Beer sells by the case,
by the wheelbarrow,
by the back hoe.

The post office knows the only
secret comings and goings here.
Only the postal clerk knows of a love far away
or an account in Panama.

The rest talk only of mechanics,
which axle broke,
who threw the first punch
and who went back to rehab –
all the way over in Bangor –
where all those big deals get made
and there is a mall to shop at
and everybody thinks they're a big deal.

This is Milo Maine.
The biggest deal here is on Bud Light
at the Tradewinds grocery store.

Blemish

He grabbed at my face to get a look,
aggravated that my teenage skin
was asking his checkbook
for yet another deductible.

She was very kind about it and
just wanted me to have some relief
from at least one of the fires
burning me up.

It didn't seem to him
that there was any conflagration
in my red and ashamed grimace.
But there was a lot of pain
that spread itself across my body
and up into my mind.
I don't remember where it hurt worse.

So I hold this memory –
of my cracked and fragile display –
to decide if I warranted the money.
And I'm left now with shoulders
thick with scars from all the worry
that could not be contained by my body.

He wouldn't remember any of this.

I'll never forget.

Confidence

It's not in the blustery wind of words.

It's in the slow grinding
forward of muscle and bone
against the weight in front of you.

Deceptive bastard he is.

You only see him
in the rear view mirror
giving you a small wave
as if to say
"Go on now."

Shoulders

He was farm boy strong,
worked hard all those years,
burned his shirts,
pulled his muscles
from the tendons
holding them in place.
He punished his joints,
sunburned his face
into a topographical map.

She is tiny by comparison –
never seemed to do much.
She smokes
hand-rolled cigarettes.
He rolls them for her
by the hundreds.
She blows the smoke
into the fan
sitting in the window
of her tiny attic room
winter and summer.

I can see now
that the whole entire thing rested
on her tiny bird shoulders.

Everything Bagel

The locomotive conversation
in front of me
between the excited woman
buying a bagel
and the bird
of an old woman
who collects the money
for the bagels
was very long,
and did not include
the topic of bagels.

My conversation
with the woman
who collects the money
for the bagels
contained only these words:
everything bagel,
veggie cream cheese,
small coffee please.

While I wait in line
I'm a bit of an impatient huffing ass.
When I finally
have the everything bagel to eat
I think about what an ass I am
and it ruins the taste of my bagel.
You can't have everything
even when that's what you paid for.

New York City Part 2

She was a tiny Jewish girl from London
and she was in love with me.
When I say she was tiny
I mean she was small
as a bird bone
but she was no chicken.
Her father had money so the view
had three sides – one on the park.

We made love like bees
high in a nest
with the windows tall and un-shaded
for all the famous people of the city to see.
We stayed up in our crow's nest
looking straight down Madison Avenue
and I picked out a building
to be my favorite –The Carlyle Hotel –
because I'd heard of it
and it had some nice copper turned green
the way copper does.

I wanted to be in love
but I wasn't.
I don't think she wanted to be in love
but she was.
I was stronger then
and my muscles were hard.
I tried to be in love
but north is north
no matter where you wish to point yourself.

Sometimes we made ourselves go outside
to the rest of the world
which seemed smaller than our nest.
We made some nice memories
of a film
and her favorite band
and a great salad.

We drank too much and sometimes
after we made love
I would watch her sleep
and my heart ached like a broken thing
to see her – fragile as a sparrow.

I watched the city below
unable to find peace
with what I couldn't keep in my heart.
It just wouldn't stay put.

If My Best Days Were Past

If my best days were past
and I were sure –
I would load the chamber
and head on back.

But I have more questions first.
And I love to take a long swallow
to fill the hollow space
that asks – what next?

And so what is left of my thirst
keeps me digging in the dirt
and wondering
what bone can be unearthed
and stacked and labeled
to explain the "why?"

The story becomes richer
as the bones pile higher
and makes me wonder even more –
what monster am I?
When all the piling is piled
and all the measured miles gone by…
What monster was I?

God

If there is a god
he's not taking your requests
like a cover band.
He doesn't care if your team wins
the Super Bowl.
He's not listening to the Christians
asking for the death
of the queers.
He's not listening to the radical Islamist
asking for the death of America.
And he's not listening to the racist
asking for the death of the blacks.
He's not taking requests
like a shitty cover band
and he doesn't play "Margaritaville."
He's hanging his head
when someone yells for "Freebird."
And he's thinking –
"These assholes don't deserve
me even playing this gig.
When can I go back to the hotel?"

When the Last Guest Leaves

I stumble around slightly drunk –
a June bug in the porch-light.
I make a small attempt to put things in place
so that the morning won't feel cluttered.

There is a hollow place inside
where the words were sitting
before I said that stupid thing to her,
and outside a thin grey sheet of clouds
tucks in the moon and sky.

Things get sorted out.
I turn the TV on to my own annoyance.
I find a thing someone left
and resent that I'll have to work out its return
and think,
"I'm not sure which I resent most,
the company of others
or their leaving me stranded here alone
with my itchy thoughts about them."

I pick things up and set them back down
until I feel I'm punished enough
then I go lie in the bed.
As the waking fades into sleep
a small tense thought roots its way in and I think
I wish I liked myself just a little bit more.

My Favorite Film

The years behind me are the shed skin
of a snake.
I can see the general shape
and the details of a moment or two.
But mostly memories are translucent
like the shed skins.
Sometimes a distinct memory comes back
in a conflagration of scent
and the orange yellow blaze of emotion.
These are diamonds –
rare to find
then they glimmer and burst
from the dirt.
The small tight curve of her waist
when I first put my arm around her,
the leather of her thrift store belt
against my forearm.
A Patti Griffin song was playing.
We were in the basement
of the house I would later move her into.
Her clothes – the smell of left
too long wet in the washing machine
then dried later
when you remember they are waiting for you.
The entire film reel is maybe 30 seconds.
But it is better than any movie I've seen.
Better than The Godfather
or Citizen Cane.
Nothing happens in my movie.
Everything happens in my movie.

Sunday Best

We shined our shoes.
We tied our ties.
Girls wore white stockings
and pale yellow dresses.
We stood in line and crossed our hearts
in our Sunday Best.

The good dishes came out and the silver too
and everybody stopped cursing
for a couple of hours.
Even the Corningware got blessed.
We were in our Sunday best.

That's good enough, he said,
I'm not trying to build the Taj Mahal.
Just a couple coats then let it dry…
Outside the snow began to fall
while he stood with paint spattered on
his one good shirt.
He was working in his Sunday best.

It's been such a long time
since my collar was that tight
and there was spit in my hair
to keep things in order.
And my shirts were ironed
and pants were pressed.

Uncle Louis is long gone now
and so are Alma and Edna
and Arthur and Lois…everybody's gone.

They were all a bunch of drunks I guess
but they did their drinking in their Sunday best.

It's dark so early these days
and roads are sanded and salted.
It's like the sun went away to dream
and the birdless sky is forever.
Jesus Christ it's so damn cold
and yes it god damn is
and those neighbors
better watch that dog
if they don't wanna get arrested.
From the screen door, wearing our Sunday best
we watched the cruiser drive away.

She Fell

Her bruised knees
and lowered eyes
tell.

She ran to my bed
but on the way she tripped
on the intimacy
that was waiting there.

And now she is sore
and waiting for the injuries
to heal.

I didn't shove her
but I didn't lean
in to slow her either.

And that's on me.
I reached out,
caught her falling
when I should have
put something in her path
before she fell.

Coffee Shop

Vanderbilt girls
with ripe asses.
The sun has done a fine job
with his work here.
One small touch
of the fruit
and it would fall freely.

The rich dark smell
of ground coffee beans
hangs dancing in the air
with the expensive shampoo
she used to clean
last night's secret from her hair.

I'm just a reporter here.
I'm only taking notes.
I'm only sitting in this garden
for the coffee.
I've already brought my harvest in.
A long time ago.

I Have Never Wanted Children

I have no children.
And so I don't worry about Legos
in my barefoot night time walking.
There are very few stains
on things in my home.
I do not catch many colds.
There is no candy in the house,
or cookies either.
I've never watched a school play.

I will not have to pay
for anyone to attend college.
I don't worry
about my daughter's safety
or the secret hearts
of the boys she has as friends.
I'll never have to clean up
after my son's hangover.
There are no children's music CDs
that play on endlessly.

Also, there is very little crying at my house
almost none – unless
I watch To Kill a Mockingbird or
finish another Jim Harrison novel.

But I have an ex-girlfriend.
And she has a baby daughter.
And when I'm around the baby –
sometimes
I think to myself

I wouldn't mind much at all
if she spit up on me,
left her Legos on the floor
or gave me a cold.

That Elusive Song

The next song –
I'm diminished by its not-yet-ness.
The song that rises
fully formed, mysterious and instructive –
a gift for all to wonder.
A melody so seductive and preternatural
that your skin raises in bumps
at the chord
that comes from nowhere but could be
no other chord –
to catapult you up
and away
inside its sacred trajectory.

That elusive song –
the next song.
A lyric so poignant in its truth
and in the poetry of its telling
that your heart will leap like a fawn
trailing its mother into the dark wet woods.
Follow me…
That elusive song.

I stood in front of the Vermeer
my eyes ponding for its impossible beauty.
Stunned and choked by the simple fact of it.
That a man could create this thing,
and I thought – "this."
I want the hand of God
to spirit my own arthritic hands to do this.

A Note to My Younger Self

You, yes you, Dorian Grey in reverse.
Just do this one thing for me:
Work harder and faster
so that you can reach the sweet apple sooner.

Work your callused hands
against the hard bark
and fucking crawl out there.
Trust the branch
in spite of its Halloween creaking.
And with your fingertips
touch the bright red thing
and pull it
to you.
Bite hungrily into it
and let its juice run freely
down your face.

It is that good – the thing you desire
is that good.
I'll be waiting for you here – hurry…

An Old Friend's Father Has Died

Big. Wicked smart.
An Atlantic crashing wave of hair.
Expensive school and
something to inherit.

There seemed something Kennedy about him
in spite of the Harley Davidson
forever partially assembled in the basement
with its lack of gasoline or spark.

He was steely-eyed and distant
in an easy way.
As if to say, good to see you –
now be careful walking home.
This was many years ago when I was a kid.

Turn pages:

He took his collar off.
Filled his glass.
Drank deeply from a new life
while the hubcaps of the life
he had driven for so long flew off
and into the gutter.
Old love made new.
He sang "A Boy Named Sue" very loudly.
Branches burned in the blaze he set.
He stomped a few embers out
with his big boot but he was finished
with his fire watch.

The last I remember
was that even with the fading
of the light in his eyes
still there was more
love, compassion, interest, questioning,
more –
than back when he was a Kennedy
having lunch with the mayor
and keeping the barking dog in his head quiet.

Questions with Coffee

Was Bukowski that good?
What is the best time of day to write?
Will I get audited?
Who will be my last lover?
What is this pain in my left elbow?
Is time simply some strange math?
How much would it cost to add cable tv?
Does Anna Kendrick have a boyfriend?
Who was William the Conqueror?
How long until I retire?
Should I off myself?
Should I relearn long division?
Does the roll go over or under?
Does your head stay alive for a moment
after the Guillotine?
Baby baby where did our love go?
What becomes of the broken hearted?
Mikita or Dewalt?
What does it smell like on the moon?
How much time do I have left?
What is my sperm count?
Should I have been an actor?
A doctor? A welder?
Should I rob a bank?
Who is the best actor pound for pound?
Chicken or fish?
Are the wasps asleep?
How long ago did I love her?
What's on tv?
Should I buy a cabin?

Is there a bird that eats wasps
and where can I get a few?
Do you know the way to San Jose?
Who invented coffee?
Is there more coffee?

If I Were a Tiger

I would lie about in the shade.
Every tight muscle would stay relaxed
and
only
when
I
explode in all my fiery orange
to sink my teeth into the neck of a young gazelle
would I move.

Then I would devour her slowly,
licking my great paws
and smacking my long tongue as I fill myself.

Then back to the shade of a yawning strange tree
to wait...

At the Tire Shop

The slow drip Tennessee drawl tells me
the tire stem done gone bad
and there's a nail in there.
Oil change won't add much time.

"Is that a Michelin? Eleven hundred
out the door.
Yes sir, be 'bout three hours."

"You get that girl's message?
That little girl works for me.
All worked out dinnit?"

Gatorade cooler has water.
Thermos has coffee,
powdered milk if you want it
and sugar too.

"Ain't in no hurry.
How's it going?
I need a rotate and balance."
"Be 'bout two hours.
Make herself at home we get you fixed up."

"Mr. Perry?
We gotcha all fixed up.
You ready to go."

Back at home
these men have enormous television sets
and camouflage coats
and carpeting
over hardwood floors.

Under their fingernails
is the bluish stain of oil
and grease that will never fade,
even in old age when
the television's picture
starts to blur
and the football game
is a wash of colors (always orange)
that leads to a deep sleep.

"Yes sir we'll get you taken care of."

And they tithe
and root
and dream
and get you all set to go.

A Little Bit of Knowledge

My brother lit the match.
To show me how
the skinny paper stick jumped to life.

Then he panicked
and threw the fire from his hand.
It landed silently on a white ornate doily
spread out on the dresser
of ancient Mrs. Meyers'
ancient bureau.

Our mother
had taken the feeble
and angry
old woman in as a boarder.

Mrs. Meyers' doily started to burn.
We both panicked.
The panic has erased
what happened next.
The house didn't burn down –
though the doily did sustain some damage
as did my brother later on.
A little knowledge
is dangerous to children
and doilies.

Jennifer

When she was young
she complained to her father
that she had inherited his over-ripe lips.
"You'll be happy for them later on," he said.
He was right.
He didn't know how happy
I would be for them.

She wore sweaters
like girls from Vermont do
and her hair was very long
and brown and beautiful
the way it moved with her.

She was quiet and shy to the world
but her secret self was
a devilish lustful thing.
Men like me know about women like her.
It's not the painted woman trying so hard
to sell you.
Need and desire are not the same.

I had a young heart
still dark red and strong
filled flush with the sweet rainwater
of hope and discovery.
Drink!

I dropped my mask for the first time
and showed my scars,
ruddy face,
fragile bones –
all that was covered and propped up
by the animal loins of youth.

An absolute marvel of a woman.
A silent arrow sunk deep in my heart.
Even now I find myself grateful for those lips
and the dish she set out for me.

Savings Account

The young grab at life
like it comes at them
on dollar bills.

The middle-aged pace themselves
waiting for a twenty
to float by.

The old give
it all back again
one dollar at a time
in birthday cards
from Walmart.

God in His Slippers

A June bug hurls itself
clumsily into the screen door
lands on its back
and flails like a tipped over wind-up toy.
A twelve-year old girl
in a Chicago suburb listens
for the footfall of her step-father's
shoes in the dark hallway
that leads to her bedroom.

A photographer hired at great expense
for an extravagant wedding
clicks away at a camera with no film
as the bride beams with happiness.
A Guatemalan boy boards a plane
with balloons of heroin in his body.
One of the balloons was tied in haste.

A dry blade of grass catches fire
from the cherry of a cigarette
thrown out the window of a Pontiac.
A baby laughs
at the spinning wheel of colors
above her crib.

In Las Vegas sand blows
across a flyer advertising
the services of an escort named Misty.
No one hears the tiny tick tick
of the grains of sand dancing
across Misty's face. Tick tick tick.

A teenage boy blows gently
on his grandmother's feverish forehead
as she reaches in vain –
too weak to pull the oxygen mask
from her face.
It's so hot… It's so hot…

An acorn pushes its root
out into the dark rich soil
then grows undisturbed
for two centuries
while June bugs careen past it
in search of screen doors.

Ready

I can feel it beginning again.
It's been a very long time.
But my arms have been feeling quite empty.
And they might be ready to bear
some weight again soon.

The last time was many years ago.
And my friends did not approve.
She was too young for them,
though since they did not sleep,
work or live with her
I don't know why her age mattered.
They disapproved anyway,
though we had a very kind
and playful private life
that we both enjoyed.
She was lovely.

But the next time will be different
and partly defined
by the age I am now.
I still have plenty of stringy lust.
But I'm quieter now.
And I no longer come close
to losing a finger in rage when
I'm wrestling with hammers and saws.

And I think it would be nice to
simply sit here with someone reading
beside me.

And someone to laugh at my jokes
would be nice as well.
I'd like someone to combine
treasure chests with
and then we could run our toes
through our golden coins.

Outside the door
there are thin green vines making their way
up the fence posts.
They hold on very lightly,
conserving their energy for growing longer and
covering more area –
not for choking the fence post.
This is a good sign I think.
And I can feel it just now beginning again.

There's Always Tomorrow

Some days
the only thing
keeping the gun
out of my mouth
is that I like a good story.
So I'm waiting
to see if my life
has some more gripping
chapters coming up.

Some days
I settle for one good sentence,
or a metaphor from the muscle
of Mary Karr's wiry forearm.

I figure I'll know
when it's time –
when the story really goes off
the rails and I think –
"I don't like any of these characters anymore,
and I don't care what happens to them next."

There's always tomorrow.
Until there's not.

Perspective

A wall could be one thousand feet long
and ten feet high
and made of bricks
and if it's perfectly straight
and you are staring at it
from its end
very close
all you will see
is a ten-foot stack of bricks.

Sailors knew the earth was round.
The top of a land mass appears first.
A ship's body disappears before the sails.
The guy in the crow's nest could still wave
goodbye
while the guys below
were peg legging around
and getting into the rum already.

When I was six years old
I hopped ecstatic on one foot
down the hallway
of a rented house
the other foot covered in dog shit
because they bought us
a puppy for Christmas.

Merde de chien!

Flight Attendant

Please keep ringing the bell,
because she smells marvelous.
And when she floats by
all hips and berry brown arms
in her sleeveless blue uniform
she brings a full sail of her scent
with her
and I breathe it in like good wine.
She might be made of honeysuckle,
or maybe that word just looks right –
or possibly both.
It could be she's made of lilac.
Please ring the bell again.
I need more
of this sweet dark drink
she's serving in coach.

First Wife

I loved her.
The way you do
when she maxes out your credit card
and blows a bartender
in L.A.
on the layover
of the trip you bought her
for her birthday.

His Favorite Bird

The Chickadee stays all winter long
through all that aching cold.
The cold that rattles your lungs
like a carburetor
and fights the sun
against every tiny drip from the icicles
threatening from the front porch soffit
that needs painting again.

He's a tough bird that one –
small but tough.
He's a born fighter.
God gave him a black eye to start with.
His feet are tiny brittle branches.
He's a tough little bird.
He's a fighter.
He stays all winter long.
He doesn't give up
or go off where things are easier.

That's why it's his favorite bird.

A New Lover

There is a girl in my bed sleeping
just
    barely.

Her butterfly wing eyelashes flickering
familiar and still a miracle every time.
This softness is a slowly unwrapped gift bringing
wide-eyed wonder
at the holy offering
and my undeserving acceptance.

The taste of her body and secrets
are still on my mouth.
I marvel at this carnal dance
and its melancholy after party
with empty glasses,
litter of clothing
and aches in my bones
and aches
somewhere in the musty room
where my no longer young
heart lives.

Nocturnal Emissions

A few days back I woke up fully
in the middle of the night.
And there were tears on my face
for my aloneness.

This took me by surprise
and it's a small mystery.
I seem to be alone by choice.
There are fine and lovely women who
make themselves available.

But I pull back only one side
of the bedding.
And I set the coffee maker
for only two cups of coffee
which I drink in bed alone while reading.

So where did the tears come from?
I've felt more alone
in the chalk outline of two bodies
on the pavement of dirty blankets
than I do with my one dirty coffee mug.
So this small nocturnal moment is a mystery.

I remember the flood lights were on
and there was a brightness
coming in the narrow crack
of the heavy curtain
cutting across my face.
Then suddenly – tears.

51

51, you don't scare me.
you don't even get an uppercase y.
15, with everything in its purple gym bag
and all the things that weren't in the gym bag,
scared the shit out of me.

Now I know this:
I can take a punch,
help her come,
the cut will heal,
how to put in a new radiator,
words mean
only what they cost to use.

I'm strong enough
to find the kindness,
and to not use the cruelty
that rides in on fear's wake.
That love is a sweet taste
to take in wherever it's found.

51 can kiss my ass.
I once knew 15 and that fucker was mean.
The door is unlocked so just come on in.
The coffee is on.
Or I have whiskey if you prefer, or Vicodin.

Author Bio

Rod Picott is an award winning, hard touring, singer-songwriter from South Berwick, Maine. He has released eight albums to sparkling reviews across seventeen years. Picott has resided in Nashville, Tennessee since 1994. He is single, has no children, and will help you move your woodpile as he's not afraid of snakes.

For more information on Rod Picott's work, tour dates and music please visit:

www.rodpicott.com

CPSIA information can be obtained
at www.ICGtesting.com
Printed in the USA
BVHW030447130619
550812BV00001B/172/P

9 780997 643619